KV-381-106

To David — with whose
friendship this became
possible.
With love from Caroline
14 July 1993

Poetry
Introduction
8

faber and faber
LONDON · BOSTON

First published in 1993
by Faber and Faber Limited
3 Queen Square London WC1N 3AU

Phototypeset by Wilmaset Ltd, Wirral
Printed in Great Britain by
Cox & Wyman Ltd, Reading, Berkshire

All rights reserved

This anthology © Faber and Faber Limited, 1993

This book is sold subject to the condition that it shall not, by way of trade or otherwise, be lent, resold, hired out or otherwise circulated without the publisher's prior consent in any form of binding or cover other than that in which it is published and without a similar condition including this condition being imposed on the subsequent purchaser

A CIP record for this book is available from the British Library

ISBN 0–571–16889–2

2 4 6 8 10 9 7 5 3 1

Contents

NICK DRAKE

The Self-Portrait of Anna Vondraček-Drake

(b. Prague 1904, d. London 1992)

Dressed up for a sitting with Rembrandt
in a stranger's velvet coat and old fox fur
tatty from the wars, her self-portrait
shows an old lady as an amateur
in the confusing art of light and shade;
left waiting in the camera's black box
and daydreaming within its shuttered eye,
until, surprised by the stark flash, she thinks
the moment gone, moves, and is next caught, blurred,
leaving the booth – and history – goodbye!

The Club of Amateur Photographers
of Prague recorded odder local tales;
tight-rope walkers crossing a town square;
balloonists; unicyclists; ghosts; and girls
in flowerbed hats; the negative white
winter bones beneath the summer skin;
also the wedding days, each child-bride
clutching a chaplet and her next-of-kin;
and formal sitters in the cold northlight
beneath a roof of glass, unknown, unnamed.

Maybe she was taken as a child
in a photographer's *atelier*
at an old biplane's controls, the bold
aviator (watching at her shoulder
a guardian pigeon) high above the still,
painted streets of Prague, set to depart

on her solo voyage far away from home;
no wind in her white curls or tighter heart,
and waving like an uncertain angel
lost to the clouds' silence and slow time.

The Permanent Guests

Along the esplanade the season's last
empty deck-chairs lie to catch the rain
to the starboard of a café steaming up.

The beanos came and went on wild-flower trains
for pleasure gardens, benches in the breeze,
the windless dunes and ships far out to sea,

and miniatures of money; tea and cake,
doileys and crumbs, and one day's coin to spend
on the telescope and on the photograph.

One day a year, and then the inland year.
The permanent guests stay on after the crowd
has left for home and the esplanade is empty;

the donkeys leave their circle in the sands;
the fortune teller closes up her shrine;
the floral clock can wither to its sticks.

Patience and pebbles, tea-leaves, cigarettes;
between the windows and mirrors, winter steams.
Dried flowers in the grate, rain at the pane

where Mr Blatny scribbles poetry
sheet after sheet in his own language lost
each day the forty years since he was wrecked

on this asylum island where he found
a beach of stones and shells, drank tea from urns,
and rode the ghost train round and round and round.

Cigarettes for Mr Blatny

(b. Brno ?1920, d. Clacton-on-Sea 1990)

His body was folds and twists, his bones seemed doubled
into themselves; I thought of an old toenail
ingrowing, a self-interrogation.

Translation from the Republic's rhetoric
to post-war England's accidental streets
erased his lyrics, cast him lunatic

and tongue-tied to the silence of the purge
of language, money, timetables and clothes:
a question mark uprooted from its past.

Pencil sharpener, paper knife, white sheets;
his daily faith – *my scratchings* – an oblique
testimony true as happiness

torn up each night, confessed again by day;
self-doubt runs through him like a water-mark's
shadow to betray itself in light.

The asylum's here and now absolves him,
yet in contemplation or procrastination
he still awaits *sub-poenas* by first post.

Proscribed, these high ceilings are England
but the winter garden there Bohemia-
on-Sea, arcadian, an old abode

with visitors to whom he may declare
(with the secret jubilation of the truant)
erections, bow and kiss the lady's hand.

One sultry Sunday, smoking after lunch,
twelve elder children watched us from their chairs,
the witnesses, crop haired and flicking ash.

To a stranger putting questions in bad Czech
he said nothing that might give himself away;
one answer – *yes* – agreed with all I asked.

I bribed him with gold packs of cigarettes;
he lit one from the last, his lucky chain;
hands cupped the smoke, still happy, still afraid.

To the Partisan Folk Dance Group of Czechoslovakia

Dear Partisans,
           the Queen Elizabeth Hall
was barely quarter-full for your display
of dance and music of the true Slovak.

The compère with a folder and high heels
explained each song in text-book English terms
of 'circle and digression folk motifs'
and 'tender temperament of boy loves girl'.

Enter rings of enamel marionettes
with red, red hearts on sleeves and tongues in cheeks,
wound by a key to turn and turn about;
while costumed hatchet shepherds and recruits

sang shrill and whistled out of jaws wired tight,
and waved them over with the wooing skill
of double-jointed skeletons on strings,
knees up to noses, slapping heels and hearts.

Cellos and fiddles in a music box
bowed up and down in syncopated time
to one old clarinet, and a cembalo
played by a boy with Buster Keaton's face.

And one by one the nervous soloists
entered the spotlight circle where they sang
of sunshine in the meadows of the song,
where Love in couples through the harvest arch

permits no dissidents, and banishes
the black-and-white step ballroom politics
and double agents tripping it up with sex.
As that nursery song in English rendered as

'A Little Lambkin has Commenced to Bleat',
the heart of what you did was comedy;
the rigid failure of the dictionary,
like mummers on the radio, to translate.

On a stage as shadowless you came to life
for the dark, empty rows of a concert hall
in the cold West, where few of the clappers could
appreciate the wishing spectacle

which you had studied to revive, reverse,
willing time to turn back down the roads
that lead the goose-step soldiers home to bed
and find the old smile on the youngest face.

And at the end, applause brought an encore;
like the mechanical figures circling
and waving regal hands and wooden swords
to the toy-time music of the clock upon the hour

whose calculated cog-teeth should have struck
blackout midnight in 1968,
the Kings and Queens joined hands, laughed at the joke,
and danced the last dance over once again.

The General at the Bus Stop

The General settles down to wait for dawn
in his office on the pavement. Soon the first
bus rounds the dark corner of the road,
all lights on, packed with sleepers. Travelling
is not his nature, whose four legs sustain
an early tour around the square's best haunts
(church steps, stone fountain, kiosk, tables, chairs),
and carry his slow shadow on his back
across the street at noon to pass the time.
His colleague in indifference is that old
devil the station master, tortured by
a timetable that wakes him like a fool
at the last star and in dead afternoons.
The buses never come and go on time
but somehow vanish with the travellers,
their luggage, money, perfume, stories, shoes,
with tickets to the cities or the sea,
or healers in the mountain villages;
as when the family abandoned him
to the silence of shut doors, deserted streets,
and the ravings of an undertable world –
who once walked on his hind legs and shook hands.

Dr Johnson's Bicycle

Balance
is the impossible
baffling trick
like luck
which comes at once
or not at all
true as the whistle
of a blackbird
in the leaves
before flying
into its element
of silence

and skaters
circling
backwards
while at the brink
of the rink
uncertain couples
on knife blades
as if walking on water
negotiate the uncertain
scribbled-out
palimpsest
of ice

Doctor Johnson's bicycle
a metaphysical
contraption of iron

which
puzzled
he thought you must
both ride
and simultaneously
ride yourself
making sense of faith
and nonsense
of science

But once astride
welcome to the wonder
high-wire
alone above
Niagara's chaos
nonchalant
as a fire juggler's
all-seeing-in-the-dark
Siva hands
that dance
to deceive gravity
with grace

the cogs and works
of a travelling clock
whirling out
from the still
chained
hub of Love
through palindrome spokes
to the relative
perpetuum mobile
of a wheel

turning the world's
transience

and the infinite
possibilities
of a puncture
coming down
a panoramic pass
in a rainstorm
when the front wheel
comes suddenly
free and runs
bucklingly on
before losing its way
in the distance

while I
fail to escape
the sudden
screaming
joke bone-
shaker crash
by shaping my fall
as a light
leap
to the hard ground
of common
sense

JANE DURAN

The Mere Pleasure of Flying

This has happened before:
the unlikely loading of my carcass towards sky,
a redistribution of weight
pulling up just under my arms – lifting me
over low munching things,
a scarf through a ring.

The ship leaves its harbour on spidery feet
past pine trees etcetera at the end of the promontory,
and unlikely, unlikely – alone in the air
I strengthen against the blue tonnage, the stopping,

and sweep past the tree where all fruits jangle.
The grape the banana the mango the apple
detach from their stems and hang independently.

From end to end of me, over house masses – flotillas –
the octagonal cinemas,
the glass dreadlocks of winter,
the sky feathery, layered, tumbles alongside me
not remote now. I fly

past the silent in twos, the speakers in threes
in the parks and the alleyways, on the docks and the
    gangways,
with two jets of water from dragon-fish nostrils –
an end-of-day celebration for things grounded and cornered,
all looking up, amazed and unworthy

to see me struggling in my element,
panting, held fast against the sky.

In the Science Museum

The quilted astronauts
in their space capsule
fling sideways
without hope

over the two poles
of the earth,
and a cloud of children
walking between.

River

The boat carries merchandise
slowly downstream,
past the signalling long grass.
A town is waiting
far away, drying its roofs
by the edge of the water,
calling in its fish.
The boat searches for the pale

blue and brown verticals of wood,
the families gentle on doorsteps,
and the town is attentive to the river
murmuring the motor in its mud.

The Abandoned House

So many moments of waking
when the sky of the navy
takes him away
zigzag
from the houses joined together
up the hill.
Twenty-four hours in port –
seeds in a rattle.

The girl climbs
to the top of her village.
A tumult of air
orange glazed
hems her in,
landlocked.

Turning the corner
she comes to the same wall
peeling, the long drop,
the abandoned house.
From here she can see
the boat far out,

almost invisible,
silver.

She considers her regrets.
'But yet
the streets were drowsy,
it was that time after lunch,
everyone indoors,
the shutters closed,
the geraniums seized and suffocated
by the heat,

a fountain of stillness
in the courtyard, just here
in the ailing shadow,
the buttons of my dress undone.'

Homecoming

The lighthouse beam waylays her
in the doorway of her cottage.
On the other side of the world
his ship lifts over each horizon.
He grows older
floating on the deepest water.

Then comes a sunrise
the likes of which . . .
red rugs raid the deck.

He is out alone, before anyone,
beard to the chaste wind.
Radiant and transparent
the jellyfish.

He sees the crystal working of the sea
round the island in the north
where the girl no longer
weeps and waits,
having something else to do
Saturday nights,
and the weathered sky creaks.

The Pumpkin at Halloween

My niece carried a pumpkin
down the supermarket aisle.
She rolled and bumped it
across the night for fun,
down the sticky rain streets,
though it was very heavy,
churning and charming as it was
with seedlore and threads,
held it in her arms
staggering slightly
under a streetlamp,
and put it down
outside some council flats
and sat on it. At home

she dug the pumpkin out,
peeked into its mathematics,
its seeds interminable,
its double dealing,
its wild lapping inner walls,
tugged at its sunk city,
jolted its days and weeks out of it,
tipped the darkness
from its eyes and mouth.
In the middle of its sunset land
we lit a candle for the pumpkin,
its forgotten trails,
its medallion oceans,
pored over the long words
it released on the wall.
Once the pumpkin lay in a field,
edible and quilted,
chiming softly.
Now it burns in a child's autumn,
ferocious and hollow.

Termination for Fetal Abnormality

Icing or sand?
This shoreline is sweet.
I snuggle into pregnancy
careful, canny
to keep the bubble floating,
soft loop under my belly button.

Thumb and index finger in an O
where the veins show through.
Summer's an eel
pitching, a landing seal.
I'm bleary eyed.
The purposes of the heart
smart and slide.

But now the cautious voices
have come alongside me
with the news.
The reeds have been tied together
like teepees in the wild violet
storm sky.
The further out they take you
the more I try to follow:
you come close, stop short,
turn away before I can feel
your breath on my hand.
The lamps are held low over me
as they search the river of my tongue
for your name, Ismail.

The Last Morning

for Edward Wright

Where the ground buckles
you have put your foot.
In the fading hills
a wheeling deer.

We arrange the bedclothes around you,
pale and tidy,
stiff as parchment layers,
surplices.

You lie back against the pillows,
alert another stillness
in which you are nimble,
arranging things,

coiling wet hemp on your boat,
pushing away
on the sallow river
past whistle, turtle, smoke.

Last night a deer was crazily
chasing a forest
and coming to rest
under a little pine tree,

its west-keeling
chandelier of scents,
shelter of saints,
the cool dew.

This morning the windows of your room
are open to the small streets.
A woman hangs a rug
from her balcony,

defies the fog
with dandelion yellow, dusk blue,
beckoning dumbshow.
We stagger with grief.

In your boat with high walls
there is no tilting tomorrow.
The bedclothes are already
centuries old.

CHRISTINE FEARNSIDE

On Thirty-Four Allosaur Footprints Found in Africa

'toes like a bird, teeth like a crocodile'

A hand-scrawled line
is not unlike one drawn
in drying lake mud
millions of years back.

Its run is a bird's.
It changes pace, pauses.
A big head lifts,
thinks like a predator.

Catkin

The recent gale brought me a gift
and news of neighbours hardly known.

A fluffy huddled living thing,
it lay on soil three storeys up.

I gripped it by its ribby middle
and felt it weightless, soft as skin.

It travelled to me limply looping
as unresisting as a kitten,

but struggled when I stretched it out
on naked palm for close inspection.

It folded twitching like a spring,
this city poplar's proud male member.

A March Day in the Alps

The pines are lathered up
with fresh snow-fall; it's wet
and misty as a wash-house.

Inside the steamy cloud
the tops of things appear
as waiting wads of white,

where figures move with limbs
slow-working, and their cries
fade fast along with colours.

Above us hanging smooth
somewhere are cleanest sheets,
old slopes turned sides to middle.

Skylarks For Ever!

Like something blown
across abandoned land
      with not a barn
or tree in sight they lift

      away from nests
coarse grasses hardly cover
      and ten feet high
start reeling out this song

      vibrating wings
to climb straight up the air
      until like moths
they throb against the light.

      My head's in sky
as I remember holding
      with mates in hiding
and all the ears of larkdom

      the earthbound end
of live ecstatic burbling
      tinkling reedy
the oddly-rusty squeak

      without a break
this one taking off
      when that one drops
falling silent homing.

One Sunday Morning

Inside the well-lit house
that is my aunt's own mind,

she fancied I was speaking
and thought of having honey,

so she put down her tray
and went to find the jar,

and taking off the lid
had got a spoonful ready,

when memory could give
no detail of the site

she'd left, where just before
she'd been remembering.

She laughed recounting later:
she'd gone the rounds tongue sweet

in dark and searched by feel.
I heard and tasted too.

'It's not a Pansy! It's a Viola!'

She greets me lit with worried wonder,
asks, 'Who am I?' and listens closely.
Yes, she's heard that name before
but has to laugh at being Mother.

She reasonably puts words together:
'If I live in a nursing home
I'll have a bed somewhere to sleep in.'
She's smiling wanly doubting it.

Exhausted now and saying nothing
forward looks are left to wander,
then hands remember balancing
a cup of tea, a piece of cake.

Finding fault restores her better:
she's sharp with kindly helpers bent
on cheering people, passing round
small things like plants to hold and smell.

The Prisoner

My daft old mother waking
comes to slowly in her Home.
Words politely muster

on her tongue, her little army
representing order
careless of the sense.

Walking in the garden
clenched feet go slowly.
Her voice moves ahead
witch-like in its croaking,
put on like dressing-up
to be the funny woman.

A fall during the night
broke a finger, damaged
others. She found the nurse.
In hospital they had to
bind both hands. She begs,
'Please take my gloves off.'

Alzheimer Unit

As on a rocky ledge
above a littered shore,
hand holding hand we sit

like maidens waiting tethered,
me and my old mother,
without a thought of rescue,

and judging by her calm
I think she does not see
what lies ahead of us

where helpless bodies sprawl
or uselessly stand by
like partly-chewed remains,

and some disquietingly
are struggling still inside
to get a grip on things,

their puzzlement like hers
expressed dry-eyed on meeting
blurring what I saw,

when suddenly she speaks,
a white-faced Oracle,
"It is a poor do."

Blackbirds in February

To earth bulbs fence with blades
she races carting off
her worm. An eye on me
she gets it endways, scoffs it.
A wet white blob extrudes.
She flies to a tree.

He's motionless till I pass.
In January a cold bird
did not care to be cautious.
He was tossing frosted leaves
like one of us bad-tempered
clattering unwashed dishes.

Blame

I see this still deep pool again,
its sides flat ground that's dropped away.

Dark water stands; it hardly moves
against the strong forbidding wall,

and yet the structure was designed
to bring a quick and safe departure!

I was drawn on by dread of it,
so different from the sea we swam in.

SHELAH FLOREY

Father (and Child)

On her father's infrequent visits –
Once he was inside –
She went round shutting all the doors.

His good works were done
Abroad. He was generous
With strangers.

But she was close
Looked too like him
To be forgiven.

It seemed he continued
To despise himself –
Had to go a whole world away

And nurture others
That were different.
His genes were something

He had no pity on
As her face carried
Them to the window

And crumpled –
Watching as he
Let himself out of the house again.

Here – Here's Your Jacket Back

Strange a white flag
Should still be in use
In the middle
Of so much technology.

Almost like children
At play – like
Groups of schoolboys
They troop toward us.

We signal and sign
To each other –
I put my arms up
You put your arms up
I have to search you
(We know how it goes) –
Here – here's your jacket back.

That was the best part
We were the ones
Still alive – whoever we were.

Massacres also took place –
When they said
It was time to go home
Not everyone heard.

Gulf War
February/March 1991

Lived There Many Years

The trees at the side of the house
Are higher
Than the top floor
They've grown a lot since last year.

In a strong wind their branches
Scrape the roof
The leaves appear
Fleetingly through the window.

A sudden shadow crosses the room
A kind of beckoning
On quiet days
They stay out of sight.

Must Country

The sleep thudded in her
Like an engine,
Drove up to her eyes and dragged her away.

Set her down in a foreign country
With invented people,
Or people she knew already behaving strangely.

It was a land she could never get away from –
Must always return to,
However long and sensibly she walked in the day.

Rescued from a Flood in Los Angeles

His life stepped
Into a helicopter
At the very last moment.

It had accepted
A proffered invitation
To continue.

Minutes before
It was stranded
On the roof of a car.

The water
Had been asking
It a question –

It wasn't going
To wait
Very much longer.

When something
Came out of the sky –
Not a god

Not with the power
Of divine intervention,
Only descending

As close as it could.
And a man –
Not an angel

Appeared at the door
Stood clearly
With open hands –

That proved irresistible.

February 1992

The Adversary

I think you should realize by now
Your house is going one way
And you the other.
Your house is into dust collecting,
Keeping spiders in the corner,
Feeding the silverfish –
Racing around when you're on holiday
Getting a few cobwebs up –
Nursing a little bit of dry rot
It got itself for Christmas.

It's not a place for you
To lie back in and be content,
Thinking because you set about it one day
It's going to be with you the next.
It's a battle
You're never going to win –
When you come back home
From wherever else you've been,
It's as much as your house can do
To let you in.

The Necessity for Continued Education

A bright scholar
Haunts the evening class,
The school addict, now sixty odd,
Sits before his teacher –

As he did when he was ten
Smartly answering up.
Being complimented on a good point
He relaxes in his chair.

What he found outside
Was not what he expected –
Employers unimpressed
By his skills in Latin verse.

Not many women succumbed
To his instant recall
Of obscure events.
Actually his love-making

Didn't rate a pass.
But here in this room,
Bare-windowed, a cupboard chipped
And stained standing in the corner –

Before someone thirty years
Younger than himself –
He feels mothered, fathered,
Lovered. And at home.

Towards the Spring

Just the branches reaching out
Aiming and pointing
As though they knew about direction
A place that should be gone to.

Held in themselves distance
Continuous journeys
Trekking the dark road
To greener country.

Visit to Haworth

The moors were not so high
As I expected them to be,
The signs in Urdu
Surprising to me
Pointing the way

With the English ones –
To the Brontë Falls.
A cold journey . . .
In shawls
The sisters had walked

Further than they thought,
Than they could imagine
Even in childhood stories.
Found the sun
And garlands round them.

Something Left to Show for It

We need lighted rooms
Where people can meet
Between walls
On a dark afternoon
And talk to each other.

What we also need
Is the rain on our face
The storm
To come in from –
Windows still shaking.

Being roughed up a bit
Intruded upon
Isn't always the disaster
We like to pretend –
We aren't left wondering

What was meant by it.
You could be right –
Perhaps we can meet
Some other time –
Room conversation.

It can be trickier
To deal with
Than the necessary fuss
With the umbrella –
The shout of it unfolded

Draining off in the hall.
A coat hung up
Visibly to dry –
Still redolent
Of a definite encounter.

BEATRICE GARLAND

Postcard

I saw a musk-rat nose across a pond,
nudging the reeds apart without a sound.

I saw a spider, touched by a note of sun,
shake out its net, bouncing it up and down.

I saw a black snake slipping off the road;
in the doorway, pulsing, a tiny golden toad.

I saw a white owl, baffled by the light,
bank silently and sheer off out of sight.

These things took place the day the summer went.
I noted them down, not knowing what they meant

or if anything at all had really happened;
only a state of mind in which eyes, opened

by solitude, could see the lives that other
creatures made: busy, and unperturbed by love

or hate. I pull the shutters inward, drop the bar;
but wind and dark still forage at my door.

Soldier

This land's rubbed bare by centuries of sky;
a kind of ochre scrub survives the wind. That's all.

I have to keep my whole life in a bag.
This is the minimum: one change of gear, a mug,

a knife, a toothbrush. We spend the hours waiting.
The lads play cards, or wind each other up,

laughing when someone snaps – they've scored.
Sometimes I leave the camp and walk a short way

into a burning nowhere; high up you see
a bright nib scrawl its double lines across

the blotting-paper blue; they leach out slowly
in the solar winds. At night the desert's cold:

our canvas city doesn't hold the heat
and wind can turn my jersey to a sieve.

I pull my fists up back inside the cuffs
and hold my thumbs for comfort. No one sleeps:

we're too afraid to dream, in case on waking
we have to make this journey once again.

Rain

Everything went wrong all at once.
Cold yellow light showed up the streaks
of ancient quarrels on the windowpanes;
splashes of dirty rain, a face
wiped dry impatiently, too hard,
with someone else's handkerchief:
as though the sodden sky would underline
the things we never do escape –
how protest turns into resignation,
and how, dully, we call it growing up.

The Animal

This is the creature sensed
at the edge of the garden
scratching along the fence,
stirring up the leaves
long after dark;

He's digging for something buried,
not quite located –
how his presence disturbs
the fine hairs on the skin;
changes this room.

I think he was always there,
crouched in the trees,
watching inhabited windows,
patient, getting my measure,
until he was ready

to gather himself for the spring,
the leap to the roof.
He enters a bit at a time,
assembles himself inside,
descends from the attic.

The coats hang stiff with cold;
he's turning in circles,
holed up in the grate, in the yellow-
backed chair with unravelling springs,
this animal silence.

Then shall I grow used to his ways;
stop holding my breath
to listen for voices of travellers?
Embrace him as friend, sleep
wrapped in his pelt?

The Sea

At night in the flat upstairs
the bed drums like a ship in a storm:

she groans at the weight of the water
streaming off her narrow flanks,

she leaps at each wave; unreefed
she will turn inside out in this gale;

sheets fly from the hand –
oh she is held in the palm of a wave –

then a shout as clean as a shell,
a shout as they're flung on a leeward shore.

We lie coiled on the ocean floor,
just touched by the distant wash.

Fish nudge back into caves.
The anemones stir.

Ghosts

At dusk we pitch camp
in your bed, building
small fires with words
and acts against the night.

Watching a glittering sky
we seem to sleep in turns.
Your mouth touching my ear
murmurs of waking in fright

from a region in the south,
an earth reddened with iron,
ancient silvery trees
and a house filled with strangers.

I was somewhere there –
my greenish eyes and naked
breasts already yours
but lost, or out of reach,

because you saw your wife
with an importunate man
wanting her to lie down;
using as argument

the transience of life,
the beautiful, unsummoned
accidence of desire,
the devices of the heart.

The moths fly up in alarm:
a man I was married to once
fingers the arm of a woman,
agreeing with all she says.

These days I live like a nomad –
no rings, no ribbons, shorn
of the weight of a perfect future,
remembering all I've learned

of dowsing for water, curing
a fever, using a flint,
of being a woman for man;
but knowing no embrace

nor fire will do to stem
the rising in the throat
when those antic figures
lurk at the edges of light.

Herculaneum

Sometimes at evening she'd climb the unwalled steps
on the edge of town, gazing across flat roofs
to the mountain, watching for his coming home
against the sun, half lost in olive groves.

This was when they were young, when she'd still weep
for nothing: the fall of a delicate flask, a flood
of perfumed oil that could turn the blues, the greens
on an intricate mosaic floor to serpents' blood.

That was the time of life when sundials worked,
the gyroscope was balanced on the pin;
before all movement stopped and in the sulphurous air
the umbrella pines ignited one by one.

The Drum: A Ballad

Dreadnought father,
felled at a stroke.
Inside your head
something broke.

The congregation
held their breath;
your voice grew slurred
and the Lesson said death.

The stretcher bore
you like an oak:
everyone stared,
no one spoke.

They drilled a hole
right through your skull,
but the spirits muttered
all's not well:

one eye open,
the other eye shut,
that mighty head
had split like a nut,

and the serial sevens
ground to a halt,
as a last axe blow
cut off thought.

It took eight bearers
all their strength
to lift the box
that held your length.

A great wind carried
away the sound
as the coffin lurched
towards the ground.

I dream at night
you're back again,
clear as sunlight,
right as rain.

I try to speak,
to catch your eye,
and same as always
you stride on by.

What did you leave me?
What did I learn?
That your heart can be broken
but your mind's your own;

that till the jolt
of the final nail
there's this drum in the body,
there's this fife in the soul.

JOHN GOODBY

In the Tropical House

The butterflies seem to hatch behind ears,
from hair – the Constable, Paris Peacock,
the Lacewing – as we stray under dripping glass;
you perhaps seeking the White Tree Nymph,
me in attendance on a Bamboo Page.

They might conjure up any possibility,
Magellan's Birdwing, Dark-veined Tiger,
Common Mormon, Postman, Mocker
Swallowtail, as they lazily settle on leaves
or open their Books of Hours in the shade.

Yet the feather-pronged moths would never feed
in the adult stage. Despite their eye-spots
and snake-headed wings, the Giant Atlas,
the Monarch and the Indian Moon Moth
could look to no future except love and famine

Was the Owl Butterfly a butterfly at all?
You might be a Painted Jezebel on the bridge
above the toy waterfall. I consider it, still
alighting from or on those harder names:
Red Pierrot, Sulphur Emigrant, the Great Duffer.

Harriet Smithson's Juliet

I

We were both slaves to the Ape of Genius,
an irlandaise and her fool. Who succumbed
to whom? By Act Three I was breathing hard;
an iron hand had squeezed my heart (O for a heart
of iron!) to the pulp of a poperin pear
before I blundered out through Le Tourneur's
alexandrine fog. Satan had sent Shakespeare,
but for once no one asked for a refund.

I would play Hamlet myself, true; sulk over
The Loves of the Angels; be translated
to dewfalls, citrus dusks . . . I was a lover
then, and stank, and wore clogs carved from firewood,
and dreamt of conducting cannonades,
of hurling myself on kettledrums. Episodes
in the life of an artist? Try more mustard,
leeks, bread, oil, salt, vinegar, cheese and lard.

II

That gentleman with the eyes that bode no good
was a sham ballox burning at my stage-door.
When Romeo kissed me, his brouhaha would
upstage the monument scene with a scene in the stalls;
when I told him flowers were homage enough
he whinnied, white-eyed, and gnawed at his buttonhole.
When the manager saw that he flapped our contract
at us, declaiming it like the Riot Act.

III

At this time I lost the power to sleep
(it is a power, as you will discover when
you lose it yourselves). Alright, so I did sleep
occasionally. But only three times. Four then.
One night near Ville-Juif on sheaves and stubble;
once, in daylight, in a field outside Sceaux;
once, in the snow, beside the frozen Seine
near Neuilly. And last, at a zinc-topped table

in the Café du Cardinal, Boulevard
des Italiens, where for five hours the waiters
dared not approach me for fear I was dead.
One power was still left me – to suffer –
and I marched to the scaffold for her murder.
A sour wineglass shivered in a homeless key;
the dawn-breeze woke. Awnings drummed. A viola
descending the Alps sang Ireland in Italy.

The Kalif of Connemara

The Tree of Life, they said, puts down twin roots
through Ibn Al-Bawwab and the Book of Kells;
beneath Galway boughs their last hookahs fumed
as they praised the Berber ululations of *sean-nos*.

Lateen-rigged *pucans*, we were told, would bear us clear
of Jabal Tariq, sea-courses set
trine by their stars – Rigel, Aldebaran, Altair –
to make a landfall beyond Byzantium.

Like ours, their Paradise is only for men.
Curd-fleshed *houris*, their virginities renewed
immaculately forever, attend each silk divan
beside spring-waters fluent as Mozarabic weave.

We are sick of turf-smoke under thatch, weather-
agues, vinegar wine and black-faced priests;
the *shamrukh* is the sceptre of empire;
Saint Patrick was our first imperialist.

We shall return to the Land of the Fathers;
our mackerel will shoal into flying fish;
The Martyrology of Tallaght's seven monks
will be embalmed in Coptic nard and frankincense:

our women may take the veil. We have embarked
cured beef, oatmeal, water-skins, pigs, and poets
to explicate *immrama*, with a guard
of Sligo Dragonskins. The people have danced

a battering for hours through to this last dawn.
I trace the *Bism'illah* on my cruciform brooch
hearing our dolphin-escort cry out from the Shannon
Issa, or *Iosa*, it hardly matters which.

Eighteen Eighteen

'What a thing would be a history of her life and sensations.'
— John Keats, *Letters*

Her breath of rampion, quids and old middens,
shrivelled him like a Sybil's breath as she bent lower
from her pole-slung kennel borne by two handmaidens
in their worse than nakedness of the Irish poor.

'Kates? Keats? Yeats? Yates? It must be you I seek,
poet, although your gyre has not yet unwound':
suddenly she pissed fit to lay the summer dust
six miles from Bangor to Donaghadee.

'I am Ireland,' she crooned, 'great is my bladder.
Know that the second Jew is come this year;
his marks appear plain in the pikes of Down
and Antrim, the lost, third strike of the weavers,

and in the Belfast Shuttle's disgusting noise
that will weft and warp the world.' She was squab,
half-starved from scarcity of biscuit, an ape
from Madagascar shipping for the Cape,

who eyed the Scotch mist over Ailsa Craig
for some clearer sign. 'Your voice is Yola,
and although you wear the butcher's apron
you stain it in the service of Apollo.

Weep subversively. There will be no more truth
until Dunluce Castle goes down on its knees
to the tides and the Sea's Swallow, until
we bury each twisted weasel's mislaid tooth;

take your text from our totem poles that spell
GOD IS LOVE by THE WICKED SHALL BE TURNED
Into HELL, take it all with a pickle o' salt:
until then I remain the Duchess of Dunghill.'

He bowed. She spat tobacco-juice: whistled, lurched off
in her sedan. His friend turned to him then
and saw his silent howl widening as if
standing for 'Christ's Entry Into Jerusalem.'

In Saint Ambrose's

after Giusti

Excellence, though you think me anti-Austrian
when my targets are fools and turnip-heads to refer
to the slurry of Danubian jakes, dilate
on the unnatural fondness of Magyars for their mares,
listen: idling in town one parched forenoon
last week (minding other people's business
for you) I happened to slip into Saint Ambrose's,
a crumbling old chapel just off the piazza

(Don't ask why. I was gooseberry for the day
to a son of that Santo the novelist who wrote
I Promessi Sposi, a work your Excellency
looks as if he's never read. Never *heard* of?
Profound apologies. No, it's a bagatelle.
Your Excellency's mind – God grant His servants
ineffable peace and a sense of proportion –
is engrossed by more than mere literature).

It was like a barracks inside. Every rank
from general down to drummer-boy was there, each one
of them an Austro – Bohemian or Croat
espaliers stuck here in God's own vineyard –
all at attention, ramrods up arses, tow-
moustached faces stiff as spindles, eyes Front!
as if God Almighty were court-marshalling them.
I kept the wall; but I wasn't wary enough

to keep *this* buttoned. One good gulp and the dry
heaves hit me (your post spares you such indignities),
though mercifully I was unbreakfasted. *Why*?
Because of the sudden stench of horseblankets,
greased puttees, cabbage soup, the biscuity sweetness of
    sweat,
because – beg pardon Excellence – in that house of God,
even as the host blanched in its elevation
the beeswax candles seemed to drool and stink of suet.

But, as the monstrance dropped there was a strange
apologetic wheeze under the altar;
an oompah band! Cornets. Fifes. A paunchy tuba.
A brass and silver burnishing of note after note
from ploughshares beaten out of swords of song, the voice

of a people suppliant in their tribulation –
you know, that Verdi chorus the Lombards chant
to Heaven, proud, unslaked, sorrowful, that 'O Lord,

from the Houses of our Birth' (the one scored
on our hearts in our Italian Babylon . . .)
It transported me. I lost the thread of myself
in the blind gripe and backwash of the thing:
as if it had made those untouchable others
people of our people, flesh of our flesh, I swayed
and blundered deeper into the crowd. Unnerving
isn't the word for it – though, granted, the piece is fine,

is *ours*, was well performed – for the way great art
occasionally transcends honest-to-goodness
bigotry. Even as the dying fall shivered
the nave my prejudice returned, sure as quails
in spring from the sea. And *then* out of those mouths –
mouths like the blond mouths of dormice – one last
chorale began to slowly creak itself aloft
through the red-eyed smokes of myrrh and sandalwood,

a bat-winged, crepuscular lament, beseeching
adagio; loam-ecstatic, fir-resinous, reproachful
as those songs that cost you your childhood, the cud
the heart chews when tears are its daily bread,
as riddled with sadness for a sister, a mother,
as gorgonzola is with mites. Divine harmony,
how could you work against such a stubborn grain!
Rapt, giddy, drunken, dizzying, it trembled

to a close; and the after-*râle* made thought tender,
fortified its iron over an anvil's beak.
And I knew: they've all been uprooted by a Hapsburg
so shit-scared of his wops and woodentops cutting loose
that he starves them, press-gangs them, whips them here
like slaves to keep us as slaves: he herds them down
from Croatia and Bohemia the way flocks
are herded south in winter to the Maremma.

What's their life after all? Rations. Drill. Floggings.
The leper garrisons where RSMs terrify
more than we ever could. The gagged mechanics
of imperial plunder (and not one blackened
scudo of it greases their palms), they hardly know
it happens. We trade them hate for hate; we whet the blade
of divide and rule, fret out the paranoid jig-
saw that carves out our leaguing against the king.

So call me bleeding heart; I pitied them. Forlorn,
loathly – when who knows but that deep down they're not
thinking 'Stuff the Emperor' too? And I swear
if I hadn't suddenly barged out at this point
I'd've turned and bear-hugged a corporal stood
right where you are now, with his hazel swagger-
stick jammed under his oxter, his dusty boot-heels
kissing. Bound fast to the stake of himself.

RODDY LUMSDEN

Vanishing

Inside the box, her heels escape the air.
He hears the hollow silence, turns to where
The blades are catching all eyes in the hush.
His click of fingers touches off a rush
Of cymbals. Now he holds the first blade taut
And steers its whetted edge toward the slot.
She slips out of her costume, checks her face
As he reveals the white dove in her place.
She lingers till the last of the applause,
Collects her things, while back on stage he saws
Himself in half with worry, grins with fear.
The sea of faces know she'll reappear
Amongst them soon. She slams a back-stage door.
Her high heels echo in the corridor.

On Home Street

These black crosses are
The first pair of eyes
I've stared into in days.

Just as disappointing are
The paintslaps of hair,
Haphazard, at either side.

And the red nose, the grin,
Mock me. Back inside,
I try to love this new room.

I hug corners, agree to differ
With the paintwork, run
My fingers through the air.

That boy, mother on one hand,
Clown painting in the other,
Should have drawn a house.

I want a strip of sky,
A dandelion sun, a chimney
With a pig's-tail of smoke.

Twenty Haiku for My Dentist

The waiting room is empty.
The fish come up for air.
You beckon me.

Clouds through frosted glass.
Your partners, indifferent,
walk through in white coats.

Around me, you place the bib.
I am not demeaned.
Beneath, we're human.

You leave the room to take
a picture of me. Please,
take me in profile.

The taste of metal
on my tongue. I learn
the physics of attraction.

My hand clutches
my arm a little tighter.
You talk above the whirr.

These words somehow slow
the drill as you repeat them,
somewhere above me.

The grinding drill you call
my favourite part. How did
you know? 'A rough guess.'

You are older than you look.
It doesn't bother me,
and then it does.

The outside world
has become the task. You fix
the clamp inside my mouth.

Anaesthetic. My present
self is a swirling one.
I smell your hair.

Camille Claudel,
you'd maim me, were I Rodin,
and make me think again.

Cautiously, I eye
the nurse. She makes amalgam.
No jealous sparkle.

One fact cannot escape me.
That warmth at my temple
must be your breast.

The radio holds
the room's stasis. Sweet lyrics –
Your instruments' names.

You ask me to take
a heavy bite. Peep inside
my cheek now, voyeur.

Your gloved fingers track
my lips, but never trace. Now,
come outside with me.

Your name on the plaque
outside. The pub across the street
has just opened.

With moist hands, I hold
my numb face. Winter sunlight
is claiming the street.

Reluctantly, I submit
your small signature
on the prescription.

The Sun-Inspector

'his eye twisted like the sun-inspector' – from a poem in
Ewe by Komi Ekpe

I made my will this morning, before
Sunrise. In case I must put
My finger into the hole of things.

I left my yellow car at the bottom
Of the hill. As usual.
I don't like the look of that cloud.

Look at this town again, blowing
Smog-rings. I twist my eye, one
More million miles through glass.

That tree was living last week.
I hung my knapsack on a low
Branch, and broke a twig or two.

The moon man is watching me again
From behind that bush, waiting
For the great darkness, and overtime.

Sometimes at twilight, we picnic here,
He and I, his big, pale face
Staring in the opposite direction.

This is a fine zenith. Can you feel it
In your skin? See how the orange
Bleeds an inch more into the blue.

They do not see what I see. I will not
Tell. Hold my jacket a moment.
I'm starting to feel a little warm.

Kippis

Of all things in this pothouse of a place,
It's this that's simplest. Not as if
We're told to do it. Things just happen.

I can't speak your language. Its bevelled
Vowels, its clicktrack of *K*s send me
Reaching for my pint. You try your English,

Strictly pidgin, and twist your lips around
What's more or less my name. I venture
Snow, rallying, lakes, reindeer. You nod

Politely and take another cigarette, not
Needing to ask this time. We hit upon
A Swedish film we've both seen, we order

Two more beers. I say cheers. You say kippis.
You say cheers. I say kippis. Simple.
In a week's time, we'll meet again. I'll walk

You to the corner when we're good and drunk,
We'll talk a while and laugh a little,
Then you won't see me again. It's that simple.

The Governor's Dog

I wouldn't say I'm not the man they need
but I am neither dangerous nor sly.
I thread my tongue through my remaining teeth
and try to talk their language. By and by,
they'll pull me through the streets into the court.
I dreamed of it last night: they had me tied
with yellow ropes. When I awoke, I thought
I heard a young girl's serenade outside.

It's said, next cell to mine, they keep a man
who loved the mayor's wife, and she loved him.
He knocks at times. I answer if I can
by drumming my good foot against the rim
of the bedcage. Yesterday, the thin guard
brought me in the governor's dog to take
a walk. I took the leash. Down through the yard
and through the trees, there is a shallow lake

where geese are reared. I asked the guard how long
and how far I should go. He stared at me,
he shrugged and left. I eyed the beast, a strong
broad-bellied mongrel. Far as I could see,
this was the test. What do they have me for?
They cannot know the thing I've really done.
My tracks are covered. Now the governor
wants me to walk his dog, it has begun.

You see, I know they'll watch how far I go.
Today, perhaps, the lake. I might look down,
catch my reflection shifting in the slow
drift of the water. Nearby, from the town,
a sound of bells. It may work out that way,
but something in my head is whispering.
I shuffle round, still limping. At midday,
they'll open up my door. They'll push him in.

The Bedroom at Arles

He filled up a cracked glass with hot water
from the blue terrine.
Somewhere behind him, all his enemies
were arranging a party.
He held the glass high up to his eye, looking.
The voices in the floorboards
had stopped for a while, so he painted.

'When Paul comes, I will show him
the garden from indoors.'

There was a chair for him, and a chair for Paul.
There was a window for Paul, and a mirror for him,
so that they could both see outside.

'If it rains, we can play at cards.'

Hands combing at his beard, the palette
lay like a dirty plate in his lap.
It was very quiet in the Yellow House,
but outside, it was a noise.
A noise like people coming, going.
A noise like dogs running on sand.
A noise like the iron gate swinging.
A noise like the wind on the canopies of the shops.

A noise like the Place Lamartine,
which he could not see
through the blindfold of paint,
which he could not hear
through the crescendo of brushes,
which he could not smell
through the anaesthesia of turpentine.

'When Paul comes, I will hang
my Japanese print in the scullery.
I'll wear my new cravat.'

Even when the voices in the floorboards
came back, they only said,

'A little more orange here,
a little more orange there.'

Detox

5 p.m. Mister Halfmast, I kick my
Mind toward the blues. Black
Coffee. I'll Get By. Whatever.

If you walked in on me, you'd
Find me flinching, drawing
Out the needle of my worst thought.

It's a picture that's lacking
A soundtrack. Go get me one
With a smoky sax, with a good dose

Of steel-brushed cymbals. Then,
On the way back, red wine,
Two bottles, some French cigarettes.

Sit on the floor and look me over.
Tell me I'll be okay. Then,
Get the hell out of here. Now.

Don't you see I'm the star of
This scene? Let me finish
This thing I didn't want to start.

MAURICE RIORDAN

Ghosts

I call it home: this house where I'm a guest,
in which the Sacred Heart illuminates
the bed, where still I sometimes wake in sweat,
where once I heard (but didn't see) a ghost.
My children, woken by the daws that roost
and squabble in the chimneys, come at dawn.
So I'm up, half-drugged but obliged to warm
and reassure. And quickly get them dressed.
It's question-and-answer hour, like do I
believe in Hell, was Joseph Jesus' dad.
And now, from my son: where did Grandpa die?
I tell him: right behind us, in my bed.
He looks – and I turn too, as though a sigh
must come from the warm clothes I've shed.

Rural Electrification 1956

We woke to the clink of crowbars
and the smell of creosote along the road.
Stripped to his britches, our pole-man
tossed up red dirt as we watched him
sink past his knees, past his navel:
Another day, he called out to us,
and I'll be through to Australia . . .
Later we brought him a whiskey bottle

tucked inside a Wellington sock and filled
with tea. He sat on the verge and told
of years in London, how he'd come home,
more fool, to share in the good times;
and went on to describe AC/DC, ohms,
insulation, potential difference,
so that the lights of Piccadilly
were swaying among the lamps of fuchsia,
before he disappeared into the earth.

The Doctor's Stone

The Doc, in slippers and samite gown,
serves warmed milk and honey,
rashers, wads of blood pudding,
to cure a night on whiskey.
He's telling of a trip to Achill –
how, as he squatted on the sand,
he saw beyond the ocean's rim
the bright tips of a palm forest.
He never found the spot again
but knows he glimpsed Hy Brazil.
And he takes from a leather case
a stone, the size of a wren's egg,
that three days ago was lodged
inside his kidney. He traces
its passage to the bladder
down the urinary tract
into the palm of his hand.

Gives me the stone to hold.
It is so light and real
it could well be the one
I all but wrested from a dream.

A Word from the Loki

The Loki tongue does not lend itself
to description along classical lines.
Consider the vowels: there are just four,
including one produced by inspiration
(i.e. indrawn breath), which then requires
an acrobatic feat of projection
to engage with its troupe of consonants.
The skilled linguist can manage, at best,
a sort of tattoo; whereas the Loki
form sounds of balletic exactness.
Consider further: that the tribe has evolved
this strenuous means of articulation
for one word, a defective verb
used in one mood only, the optative.

No semantic equivalent can be found
in English, nor within Indo-European.
Loosely, the word might be glossed as *to joke*,
provided we cite several other usages,
such as *to recover from snakebite*;
to eat fish with the ancestors;
to die at home in the village, survived

by all of one's sons and grandsons.
It is prohibited in daily speech,
and the Loki, a moderate people
who abjure physical punishments,
are severe in enforcing this taboo,
since all offenders, of whatever age
or status, are handed over to *mouri*

– sent, in effect, to a gruesome death:
for the victim is put on board a raft,
given a gourd of drinking water, a knife,
and one of those raucous owl-faced
monkeys as companion, then towed
to midstream and set loose on the current.
Yet the taboo is relaxed at so-called
'joke parties': impromptu celebrations
that can be provoked by multiple births
or by an out-of-season catch of bluefish.
They are occasions for story-telling
and poetry, and serve a useful end
in allowing the young to learn this verb
and to perfect its exact delivery.

For the word is held to have come down
from the ancestral gods, to be their one gift.
And its occult use is specific: to ward off
the Loordhu, a cannibalistic horde,
believed to roam the interior forest,
who are reputed to like their meat
fresh and raw, to keep children *in lieu* of pigs,
and to treat eye and tongue as delicacies.
The proximity of danger is heralded
by a despondency that seems to strike

without visible cause but which effects
a swift change among a people by nature
brave and practical, bringing to a stop
in a matter of hours all work, play, talk.

At such crises, the villagers advance
to the riverbank and, as night falls,
they climb into the trees, there to recite
this verb throughout the hours of darkness.
But since, in the memory of the village,
the Loordhu have never yet attacked,
one has reason to doubt the existence
of an imminent threat to the Loki –
who nonetheless continue, in suspense, their chant.
At once wistful and eerie, it produces
this observable result: that it quells
the commotion of the guenon monkeys
and lulls, within its range, the great forest.

Steak

Just when she thought all that was finished,
it hits her again out of the blue,
slips from her tongue like a swear-word: steak.
And she's gone, not to some wiseacre butcher
who'll fob her off with smiles and a T-bone.
To the supermarkets, where she's free to pinch
and poke, to sniff if need be. And she finds it
at Waitrose (as it happens): a half-pounder,

beautifully marbled and plum-coloured,
reduced to half-price. How that makes her laugh!

(This is no Nineties anchorite, but one who knows
the business of old: Augustine on his day off.)

Now she is home and, good, they are still out.
She opens the back door, windows, the wine.
She reddens the pan, takes the meat to warm
between her palms, then slaps it on . . .
Two minutes a side: but hot, hot, hot.
She waives the mushrooms and the onions, just
a tittle of garlic, seasonings, claret.
Does she tremble somewhat? Never mind,
no fat or gristle to speak of. She sits
in the afterglow, dandles her wine, burps.

Time Out

Such is modern life – Stephen Dobyns

The two young ones fed, bathèd, zippered, read to and sung
   to. Asleep.
Time now to stretch on the sofa. Time for a cigarette.
When he realizes he's out. Clean out of smokes.
He grabs a fistful of coins, hesitates to listen before
Pulling the door softly to. Then sprints for the cornershop.

When he trips on a shoelace, straight into the path of a
     U-turning cab.
The screech of brakes is co-terminous with his scream.
The Somalian shopkeeper, who summons the ambulance,
     knows
The face, but no, not the name or address – just someone
He remembers popping in, always with kids (this he doesn't
     say).

Casualty is at full stretch and the white thirty-ish male,
Unshaven, with broken runners, is going nowhere. Is cleanly
     dead.
Around midnight an orderly rummages his pockets: £2.50 in
     coins,
A latch-key, two chestnuts, one mitten, scraps of paper,
Some written on, but no wallet, cards, licence, or address
     book.

Around 2 a.m. he's put on ice, with a numbered tag.
Around 3 a.m. a child wakes, cries, then wails for attention.
But after ten minutes, unusually, goes back to sleep.
Unusually his twin sleeps on undisturbed until six o'clock,
When they both wake together, kicking, calling out *dada*, *dada*

Happily: well-slept, still dry, crooning and pretend-reading
     in the half-light
Till one slides to the floor, toddles to the master bedroom,
Sees the empty (unmade) bed, then toddles towards the
     stairs,
Now followed by the other, less stable, who stumbles half-
     way down
And both roll the last five steps to the bottom, screaming.

To be distracted by the post plopping on to the mat: all junk,
Therefore bulky, colourful, glossy, illicit. Time slips.
Nine o'clock: hungry, soiled, sensing oddness and absence,
Edgy together and whimpering now, when they discover
   the TV
Still on, its 17-channel console alive to their touch.

The Italian Parliament, sumo wrestling, the Austrian Grand
   Prix,
Opera, the Parcel Force ad, see them through to half-past nine
When distress takes hold and the solid stereophonic
   screaming begins,
Relentless and unusual enough to grab the attention
Of the retired French pharmacist next door

Who at, say ten o'clock, pokes a broomstick through her rear
   window
To rattle theirs: magical silencing effect, lasting just
Long enough for the elderly woman to draw up her shopping
   list,
To retrieve two tenners from the ice-compartment, dead-lock
   her front doors,
Shake her head at the sunning milk, and make it to the bus.

Let us jump then to 10 p.m., to the nightmare *dénouement* . . .
No, let us duck right now out of this story, for such it is:
An idle, daybed, Hitchcockian fantasy (though prompted by a
   news item,
A clockwork scenario: it was five days before that three-year-
   old
Was discovered beside the corpse of his Irish dad in Northolt).

Let us get *this* dad in-and-out of the shop, safely across the
   street,
Safely indoors again, less a couple of quid, plus the listings
   mags
And ten Silk Cut, back on board the sofa: reprieved, released,
   relaxed,
Thinking it's time for new sneakers, for a beard-trim, for an
   overall
Rethink in the hair department. Time maybe to move on from
   the fags.

Last Call

Home late, his house asleep, a man goes to the phone,
and from habit, expecting nothing, touches the Recall.
But this time he tenses to hear the electronic scramble,
the pause before the lottery digits fall into place.
At the other end, sure enough, he hears a male voice,
no one he recognizes, repeating *Hello, hello?*
He can hear background piano, Chopin or John Field,
establishing a room, smoke-filled, larger than his,
where wine in a discarded glass is losing its chill,
while the voice continues, good-humoured, persuasive:
Come on, say something. He tries to picture a face, a hand,
to fit the voice, still in his ear, still going on, *Last chance . . .*
He hangs up, his own hand shaking with intimacy.

The Table

Remember that table we used to want?
That we agreed should be plain, serviceable wood,
with drop leaves, to complete our tiny room.

Something to which baby-chairs could be yoked,
that might expand, in time, for supper-parties,
for renewed experiments with the spirit lamp.

Across which, over the wine and profiteroles,
we could tell each other stories: how I was thrown
off a buckrake under the back wheel of the tractor;

while you, a girl in Ontario, stuck your barrette
in a socket and were saved from electrocution
by its rubber band. You'd gloss *barrette* as hair-slide.

And we'd agree these were simultaneous events,
so we might chuckle once more at the providence
of coming together, to increase and multiply,

here, around a table we'd hunted down in New Cross,
having perambulated your bump (the twin-tub!)
through loft upon loft of displaced furniture.

We never gave up on that table, you know,
not officially. And I've kept an eye out for it,
scanning from habit the small ads and auction lists.

Would you believe me now if I telephoned
to say I'd found one? Nothing fancy or antique,
but an honest specimen of Forties joinery.

It would require work. That marbled green veneer
would have to go, along with several nicks
and gouges, obscure stains, other people's memories.

Sure – a lot of work. But you can still see
somewhere inside it the original shining deal,
the plain altar still fit for household ceremonies.

Biographical Notes

NICK DRAKE was born in Hertfordshire in 1961. 'The Self-Portrait of Anna Vondraček-Drake', 'The Permanent Guests', 'To the Partisan Folk Dance Group of Czechoslovakia' and 'The General at the Bus Stop' are included in *Chocolate and Salt* (Mandeville Press, 1990); 'The Permanent Guests' has also appeared in *Storm*. Nick Drake is also the author of *The Poetry of W. B. Yeats* (Penguin Books, 1990), and his translations from the Spanish include Griselda Gambaro's *Putting Two and Two Together* (Royal Court Theatre Upstairs, 1991). In 1990 he received an Eric Gregory award. He works as Literary Manager at the Bush Theatre in London.

JANE DURAN was born in Cuba in 1944 and grew up in the United States. After studying at Cornell University, she came to England in 1966. She taught English in secondary schools before joining the British Council in 1973 where she worked until recently. She has published in a number of anthologies and magazines. 'Termination for Fetal Abnormality' and 'River' have appeared in *Spokes*, and 'The Pumpkin at Halloween' in *Poetry Durham*. A pamphlet of poems, *Boogie Woogie*, was published by Hearing Eye in 1991.

CHRISTINE FEARNSIDE was born in Yorkshire in 1929 and educated at Cambridge University. She has taught English as a foreign language, and in 1984 began to write poetry. 'A March Day in the Alps' first appeared in *Envoi*, and 'Blackbirds in February' in *Pennine Platform*.

SHELAH FLOREY was born in Somerset and brought up in London, where she has spent many years working in offices, while writing plays and short stories. She received an award in the London Writers Competition, 1988, and has published a pamphlet *Mostly about People* (Camden Voices). Other poems have appeared in *Aireings* and *Envoi*.

BEATRICE GARLAND was born in Oxford but has lived most of her life in London. She read English at Cambridge University. After having a family, she retrained and now works in the National Health Service. She has two sons, and a step-daughter and step-son. She began writing in 1989. Some of her poems have appeared in the *London Magazine* and the *Spectator*, and 'Postcard' was broadcast on BBC Radio 4's *Poetry Please*.

JOHN GOODBY was born in Kingstanding, Birmingham, in 1958, and educated at the Universities of Hull and Leeds. A pamphlet of poems, *Before the Flood*, was published by Littlewood Press in 1986. He was awarded a Yorkshire Arts Council Writer's Bursary in 1987. He was a major winner in the 1989 Arvon/Observer Poetry Competition. Since 1990 he has lived in Cork, Ireland, where he works as a lecturer at UCC. He is married and has a baby daughter.

RODDY LUMSDEN was born in 1966 in St Andrews, Fife. He attended Madras College, Edinburgh University and the School of Scottish Studies. In 1991 he received an Eric Gregory Award. He lives in Edinburgh.

MAURICE RIORDAN was born in 1953 in Lisgoold, County Cork. He was educated at University College, Cork – where he later taught – and at McMaster University, Canada. He now lives in London with his two children and works in Adult Education. He was a prizewinner in the 1991 National Poetry Competition. 'The Doctor's Stone' first appeared in *Raven Introductions 4*; other poems have appeared in *Oxford Poetry*, *Verse*, *Poetry Review* and *Poetry London Newsletter*.